CRAZY
ABOUT
WOMEN

CRAZY ABOUT WOMEN

Poems
by
Paul Durcan

The National Gallery of Ireland

to

K

Beauty is the harmony of chance and the good.

- Simone Weil

Published by The National Gallery of Ireland
on the occasion of the exhibition
Crazy About Women
at The National Gallery of Ireland
15 October - 20 December 1991

Reprinted October 1991

British Library Cataloguing-in-Publication Data

Durcan, Paul, *1944-*
Crazy About Women
I. Title
821.914

ISBN 090316258X Pbk
ISBN 0903162598 Hb

Photography by John Kellett
Produced and Designed by Creative Inputs
Colour Reproduction and Printing by Nicholson & Bass

Cover:
Man With Two Daughters
Giambattista Moroni (c.1520/25 - 1578)

Acknowledgements

Though many of history's most celebrated artists drew much of their inspiration from the great corpus of classical literature, particularly its poetry, few writers have used painting as the basis for their creations. The exhibition *Crazy About Women* and this volume which accompanies it is therefore somewhat exceptional, in that it reverses the usual process. Museum visitors are frequently puzzled by what they are expected to appreciate in a painting, how to respond to art and what they are to make of the artist's intentions.

Paul Durcan's specially commissioned series of poems is one man's response to what painting means for him. The pictures he has chosen to write about cover virtually the entire spectrum of the Gallery's collections and it is evident from what he has written that for him a painting is not just a visual record of what an artist recorded on canvas, but something more vital, capable of provoking a rich and varied personal response which works on many levels, aesthetic, historic, cultural and emotional. This collection reflects the deeply personal response of the poet to the many images contained in the Gallery's collection. This response is both moving and intelligent, full of wit and passion.

We are greatly indebted to Paul Durcan for having so promptly and generously agreed to our proposal to write a volume arising from the collection. It took a special form of courage and a quick intelligence to undertake to compose a volume of poetry on such an exceptional subject. Dr Brian P. Kennedy, Assistant Director, who first promoted the idea, has worked closely with the author to see the project through to its completion. Michael Olohan and John Kellett, assisted by Paula Hicks, have supplied the photographs which so handsomely illustrate this volume. The layout was designed by Creative Inputs and Mary Gallery was responsible for overseeing the production. The exhibition was arranged by Fionnuala Croke. A final word of acknowledgement is due to Nicholson & Bass Limited who have generously supported the production of this unique volume.

Raymond Keaveney
Director

Foreword

It has been a privilege and a pleasure to be involved in the publication of this book, *Crazy About Women*. I first appreciated Paul Durcan's passion for paintings by the strong pictorial references in some of his poems, especially in his most recent volumes. But I never imagined just how intense is this passion. He quite simply loves paintings. This was evident from the enthusiastic, dedicated and humble manner in which he accepted the National Gallery of Ireland's invitation to develop his interest in a book specifically founded on the Gallery's collections.

In this book, Paul Durcan demonstrates that he is a radical, brilliant poet, and a traditional art curator. He has scrupulously placed his selection of paintings in chronological order and has given them the titles favoured by scholars. His respect for the paintings has been paramount and they have inspired an outstanding collection of poems.

During the writing of *Crazy About Women,* this passionate poet invited me on a number of occasions to walk around the Gallery with him and to talk about the paintings. The only question I was ever asked was 'How do you feel about this painting?' My answers had to be personal and subjective but that is what was required. Paul Durcan is fascinated by the potential of paintings to offer us a unique and personal relationship with a visual image. He has taught me how much I love paintings. They prompt the entire range of human emotions and provoke a different reaction depending on our mood as we view them.

Most visitors to the National Gallery of Ireland spend less than a minute before any one painting. Paul Durcan has encouraged us to stay longer, to learn more. Paintings can enrich us physically, mentally and spiritually, but to experience this requires time. These poems have the same power. Please enjoy them.

Dr Brian P. Kennedy
Assistant Director

Preface

In the summer of 1990 I was invited by the National Gallery of Ireland to compose a book of poems out of my experience of the Gallery and its collection. I accepted the invitation on the basis that the book would not be a coffee table book but a book as well-founded and inexorable as any other book of mine.

As with my previous books of poems, the origins of this book go back a long time. They go back to winter nights in Dublin in the early 1950's when my mother used take me one night a week for yet another magic assignation with Sheila FitzGerald.

Sheila FitzGerald was a painter who gave classes in her home in Frankfort Avenue. (See *A Donegal Summer*, Sheila FitzGerald, Raven Arts Press, 1985.)

To these two women - Sheila Durcan and Sheila FitzGerald - I owe my lifelong obsession with picture-making. While writing poems is what I do, my other preoccupation has always been the picture gallery or the picture house. On my desert island the books will be art catalogues and film scripts.

In 1967 I was working as a clerk in the North Thames Gas Board adjacent to the Tate Gallery. Every lunchtime I walked out the back gate under the billboard proclaiming 'Look Ahead With Gas' to sit in front of the pictures of Francis Bacon. These pictures - *Study of a Dog, 1952; Three Studies for Figures at the Base of a Crucifixion, 1944; Study for a Portrait of Van Gogh IV, 1961;* and *Portrait of Isabel Rawsthorne, 1966* - lit up the gloom of life and turned my eyesight inside out.

In 1980 I visited quite by chance R.B. Kitaj's 'The Artist's Eye' exhibition in the National Gallery in Trafalgar Square. I visited it daily for three weeks.

The Kitaj show changed my attitude to art - expanded it and revolutionised it and gave me back the authority of my own eyes. Since 1980 I have regarded painting and cinema - the experience of looking at pictures wherever I happen to find them - in the M.F.A. in Boston or in Grennan Mill in Thomastown, in the U.G.C. Danton in Paris or in The Light House in Dublin - as essential to my practice as a writer. Picture-making is the air I breathe and so, when the invitation came from the National Gallery of Ireland, it was a convergence of the two preoccupations of my life.

It is promulgated by the arbiters of culture that an artist should have only one spouse. An artist such as myself with the two spouses of poetry and picture-making is not looked upon favourably by the chaperones of art.

Let us be chivalrous to the chaperones but let us never compromise with their punitive monomania. Art is not a prison with poetry in one cell, picture-making in another cell and so on. "Spare me the ghostly procession of your conceptual categories" wrote Nicholas Berdyaev.

The challenge of art is to be inclusive and *Crazy About Women*, born out of a lifetime's romance with the National Gallery of Ireland, is my attempt to be so inclusive as to make the intercourse between what is painted and what is written as reciprocal as it is inevitable. We are all members of the audience.

Paul Durcan
1991

Contents

ST GALGANUS

Andrea di Bartolo

St Galganus

Sanctity! I have my doubts about sanctity!

Blue Rose - your boat, your sea, your whale
To guide you to your life and with you sail.
Welcome ashore to the National Gallery Restaurant,
To our gold sky, our orange trees, our limestone plateau.
Over black coffee and black forest gateau
I will point you in the direction of your life,
In the direction of Central Park.

Your family fret at the glass doors of the restaurant
As at airport departure gates - tightlipped, tearful.
They recognise that the space between you and I -
The space of a table - that it is the work of a lifetime:
The work of an artist;
As are the trees burnt into gold, and the stitched sky, and I
The far side of the table - small bandylegged seadog in punk halo.

Why should they take my word for it? For anything?
But they are taking it. Having taken you today
Out of school to vouchsafe you your heart's desire
In all its proud homesickness, all its vengeful innocence:
You who at sixteen proclaim you are a singer
And simultaneously a helper in Romanian orphanages;
Quivering adolescent - Blue Rose of Paradox.

That Sunday morning when you stayed home
From church and your family invited me to ride back
Ostensibly for lunch but in truth to confront you -
You confronted me in a rug with a cockatoo
Quoting modern American poetry,
Your adolescence spilling out all over me:
'But in contentment I still feel the need of some imperishable bliss.'

Around the reservoir in Central Park
For you bliss will unfold
Among young folk taken hostage by Aids.
You will mingle with them out jogging at dawn,
Stamping in fog. Pennies in a mould.
Brakedancing, skateboarding, rollerskating.
Blue track suits, blue training shoes, blue walkmans.

Around the reservoir in Central Park -
Park which is Central to all of life's trck -
Where we played Dead with our Mums and Dads;
Where we played Dead without our Mums and Dads -
You will meet Christ on the cross
Not cringing up there in the trees like a monkey
But staring straight out at you, offering you his hand;

Askew in his sweat-gelled hair
The headphones of his own blue Sony walkman.
The reservoir in Central Park -
As in a fifteenth century tiny Tuscan panel -
Is a bit of sky that fell on earth.
Blue Rose - come seed yourself between my knees and be
My Pasque Periwinkle - your whale, your boat, your sea.

Sanctity! I have my doubts about sanctity!

The Crucifixion

Friday afternoon, three p.m.,
Visiting my daughter in the Psychiatric Unit,
Killing time in her cubicle.
I sit. She stands. In the window.
My young hero of loneliness,
Her hands behind her head,
Her plaited dreadlocks,
Her crown of thorns,
A gold sky outside,
Half-astride the sill,
Pretty shrew in the badger's jaws.

You are my father -
Why can't you get me out of here?
Look at my knees -
Are my knees not benign?
Look at my legs - are my legs
Not sheer as nylon stockings in glossy advertisements?
The pain in my head
Has percolated down to my toes.
Father, have you never seen the waterfall at Powerscourt?
Why is it, Father, that all you can say to me is
"Tie up your hair" or
"Be a brave woman and bear it."

Eli, Eli, lama sabachthani?
I am a woman, Father,
In spite of the fact that I've got hairs on my upper lip.
Why will you not accept me for what I am -
A woman with a woman's soul - a roodscreen?
Father, why have you dumped me?

Why can't we go for a walk together in Thomas Street?
I can't imagine anymore what it must be like to be ordinary -
What it must feel like to walk along Thomas Street
And to post a letter in a green pillar box on the corner?

THE CRUCIFIXION

Giovanni di Paolo

When I tell the doctors that the palms of my hands
Are hurting me,
That I've got a pain in my side,
That my feet are bleeding from being made
To wear shoes that are too small for me,
That personality and nature are not synonyms,
They tell me that I am imagining it all
Or that it's a case merely of childbirth.
Father, have you never seen the waterfall at Powerscourt?

How right they are, Father,
Only they do not know it.
I *am* imagining it all and
I *am* giving birth to the world
In the corner of a carpark.

Father, do you see the new
Carparks they've laid out?
Open the window and take me in your arms.
Call me by that name
You used first call me by, remember?
'My pretty shrew'.
Throw out of the window
Your pretty shrew
Down into the carparks.

I want to stretch out
On the gold-paved path
In a dream of velvet loneliness
With carparks all around me
From head to toe,
Under the gleaming hub of your right front wheel.
Father, have you never seen the waterfall at Powerscourt?

The Virgin And Child

My mother is as much
A virgin at seventy-five
As she was at seventeen;
As much a small
Stream going nowhere;
As much a small
Ocean going everywhere;
Terracotta moon
In pink nightie.

When I visit her
In her apartment
In the solitary suburbs
I jump up into her arms.
She hugs me, holding me up
With her left hand under my bottom:
'O my curly-headed
Little golden wonder
What has become of you?'

Once a virgin mother
Always a virgin mother.
In my forty-seventh year
My virgin mother cradles me in her arms;
A brief trout of a frown
Jumps up
The brief weir of her face.

Mother most lost;
Mother most found.
Mother most doggèd;
Mother most frail.
Mother most peripheral;
Mother most central.

Truth is, son,
You and I as a pair
Are, were, always will be
Out on a limb,
Outcasts in terracotta;
Refugees in clay.

THE VIRGIN AND CHILD
Workshop of Lorenzo Ghiberti

THE HOLY FAMILY WITH ST JOHN

Attributed to Francesco Granacci

The Holy Family With St John

My oar is dragging and my boat
Is turning almost full circle
To drift sideways onto the family shore.
Although I am a man without a family -
A leaf in driftwood - I revel
In the human family's animal beauty.

Amplitude, ambiguity, affinity;
Horseshoe sandals, frisby halos:
Her young fellow all ebullience with his young playmate
Whose trim penis peers out like a bullfinch from a bough:
Her husband the carpenter, sweetest of men,
And his donkey, conversing with one another;

Putting their heads together, attentive to one another,
Donkey doing his alert best to believe his ears
Having stopped in his hoofprints to take it all in,
What the husband is confiding about his sensational spouse:
Her toes, her knuckles, her eyebrows:
The human family - what it knows.

I row back to Trim. I go into *The Judge and Jury*.
I drink a long slow black pint with a halo on it,
Feeling crimson with every sip, crimsoner and crimsoner,
Gold in my belly.
Back out there on the river - a pretty emotional picture.
What is it that a donkey sees in a man?

THE SEPARATION OF THE APOSTLES
Styrian School 1494

The Separation Of The Apostles

My name is John - one of the twelve
Gay men selected by Jesus.
I think he selected us because we are gay.
In the era of Aids we would be
The most appropriate ones to communicate his message
Of mercy to the world - the genocidal world.

We have been many years together and some of the gold leaf
Of our halos has flaked off but for all that
Our tenderness for one another has multiplied with the years
And as I dip my jug into the well at the gate
I can feel all my maternal love for the world
Surge in my breast and the prospect of the t.v. studio
Tonight on the current affairs programme
With the columnist from *The Irish Times* whose speciality's
Haruspicating the entrails of men with feminine souls -
The prospect does not intimidate me as once it used to.
My greatest fear would be to have been born
With the maternal feelings God gave me
But not to have recognised them. How privileged I was
To have had for a father a man who when asked what he thought
Of his eldest son being gay, he declared that he loved me.

The real pain is the pain of separation - that the twelve of us
After living together for so many years in County Mayo
In the Delphi Valley between Leenane and Westport
In what was once a shooting lodge of Lord Sligo's -
That after living together in peace and harmony and affection
We must separate. The fact is that we always knew
We were in the end on our own and that God's trust in us
Was precisely that we would never commit the lie
Of being dependent on one another - yet love one another we do.

In this most genocidal era of all, the era of man's trousers,
Cavalry twills, combats, fatigues
We are men who wore dresses:
Long flowing dresses of all colours and fabrics,
Pinks and scarlets and greens, cottons and woolens.
We wore halos also and in the long winter nights
We'd all fall silent, halos nudging halos,
Making a longdrawnout clang, a brisk clamour.
The secret to the apostolic life is dance
And today is our dance of separation
On disco floors of desert - bare feet arias.

You catch us at the Ball of our Dispersal
Fine tuned with hysteria, grief, despair even,
A moment of besieged delicacy.
The oldest among us, Andrew and Bartholomew,
Are dancing a foxtrot together,
A middle-aged couple at a Sunday afternoon tea dance,
Holding one another up,
Bartholomew being mindful of Andrew's arthritis.
Andrew suffers also from insomnia, poor man.

Young Thaddeus - watching the old pair -
Puts a pilgrim hipflask to his lips and drains it to the dregs.
I like the butterpats in his buttered beard.

Peter and James, slow jiving,
Shake hands as they break bread for the last time:
We two boys together clinging;
We two boys together shaking hands;
'Don't forget to send me a postcard from Berlin.'
'I won't - you neither when you get to Paris, Texas.'

Matthias looking over his shoulder does not know
Whether he is coming or going, whence or whither,
All fancy hat and cane;
When all is always said and done, always a song and dance man;
A bit of a dandy the way he holds his cane
And he cannot help sniggering as he goes.

Is he looking back at Simon already gone off on his own
Travelling at speed across a creek? Simon was always one
For dashing about - a psalmist on speed someone called him.
He is holding out his cane like a water diviner's rod.
James the Less has hitched his cloak to his cane and appears
About to go hang-gliding over Cong and angelic Philip -
He used to be a schoolteacher in Belfast -
Has already made friends in his new life but all we can glimpse
Are his wings sprouting out from behind a rock,
His red cloak bunched around his cane.

Thomas and Matthew are sharing a last cup of wine:
Little men with such innate good natures
Be it in the handball alley at dusk
Or at first Mass at dawn - such etiquette, such decorum:
Their choreography always a joy - such spiritual logic;
Everything so mercifully poised between them;
The line between life and death so thin;
Constantly in a state of nearly falling over.

Out front of us all on this foreshore where
The river's exaltation loses itself in the sea's desolation
The Master of the Separation of the Apostles
Getting ready to put away his paintbrushes for another night
Leaving behind him gold skies of midnight suns,
The melting, cracking sound of his mother's heart:
Her black purse thrown down on the ground.

CHRIST BIDDING FAREWELL TO HIS MOTHER

Gerard David

Christ Bidding Farewell To His Mother

Barefoot in the waiting room of the vet
Stinking of disinfectant and polish
Farewell, my sweetest mother,
Dogsbody given the run around by everybody,
I go now to be offered for the salvation of mankind
And to work for relief in the Sudan
In your turquoise nightgown, my boy's first beard,
And you to be led away by artistic guards in denim suits:

The modern solution
To the mystery of life:
To put mother down.

On balance, mother,
I think you will survive
Because I believe you will survive.

My left hand cautions me
That your salvation is hopeless:
My right hand encourages me
That your salvation is hopeful.

My right hand
Listens to my left hand
But as it listens
- In the illuminated act of listening -
My right hand makes up its own mind,
Follows its own nose.

My right hand -
Sizing up the Cake of Mercy
And taking aim,
Taking the measure of you, the sitter,
My sweetest mother -
My right hand
Aligning itself with my left foot

On the lozenge of a yellow tile -
Cuts the Cake of Mercy
At the acutest angle
Making certain that you perceive me,
That your grasses have moisture enough
To receive my blessing,
To digest my crumbs,
To endure my artistry.

'Make way, make way, make way' -
Three artistic guards in denim suits
With political tracts under their left arms,
Three identical triplets,
Trip past us up the stairs
A puff belligerently
Taking no notice of us.

Farewell, my sweetest mother,
Dogsbody given the run around by everybody,
I go now to be offered for the salvation of mankind
And to work for relief in the Sudan:

> *The modern solution*
> *To the mystery of life:*
> *To put mother down.*

Katherina Knoblauch

Papa put me up for auction when I was nineteen.
It was the happiest day of my life.

He was in such high good form.
He and Mama had been holidaying on the Danube.

All his life he had daydreamed of the Danube.
His beside book was a book called 'Danube'.

He brought back home with him a video of the Danube
And on my nineteenth birthday he threw an auction party

To which he invited all the young men
Of Kells and Trim, Carnaross and Crossakeel.

At the height of the party he called for order
While he showed his video of the Danube.

He bade me stand the near side of the screen
In my party dress with decolleté chemise.

I did not feel in the least intimidated or embarrassed
Because I knew that the man who would bid for me

Would have to be at least as daft as Papa.
I felt smug with the Danube at my shoulderblades,

Barges, and mountainpeaks sheering off from my earlobes;
Sedate cities at my cheekbones.

I knew also that the young men of Meath would recognise it
As Wicklow - all mountain and river:

That enchanted county from which we are all exiled;
Glad to be exiled from, but for which we pine.

KATHERINA KNOBLAUCH
Conrad Faber

In my black and red dress and gilt belt and gold leaf
I know that every man will desire me.

But only the daftest will take me
For what I am, a true Danubian.

On a day like today I can afford to be coy;
I who am countrywise and straight as a die.

I am an icon; a pin-up; nobody special.
My hips are the hips of a female seed-vessel.

For making me feel part of the Danube landscape
I will always adore your memory Papa:

All the cities far below and the one little tributary stream
Feeding the one big river. In the vein of my forefinger.

PORTRAIT OF A MAN AGED TWENTY-EIGHT

Georg Pencz

22

Portrait Of A Man Aged Twenty-Eight

I

The gravest genius to emanate from Dublin since Joyce -
That's what the pundits say about me although I am only twenty-eight.
What they do not know is that I will never sing again.

When I gave all those interviews, performed all those photo calls,
Put on all those recitals,
I slept every night with sleeping pills under my pillow;
Look closely at the pupils of my eyes.

II

I hold my parents in the palm of my hand.
As I sit akimbo in the snug of my local public house
'The Gravediggers'
Posing - posing - for my young German friend Pencz
- Son of my father's friend, the goldsmith Handke -
I can say over a pint of stout
Without fear of hubris or bathos or rhetoric
My parents are my sole subject of interest
And if it were otherwise, would that not be odd?

Art is private relations - not public relations.

My father works in the Department of Agriculture.
He is an Inspector of Sheep, Goats, Deer.
My mother imports oriental rugs.
What you behold here in this domestic tableau
Is my father being characteristically attentive to detail
And my mother, likewise characteristically,
Not getting overexcited, playing down his attentions,
Looking over the new haircut he has come home in;
Giving him her verdict on the parting down the middle,
A new departure for him. She is giving him
Her I'm-looking-you-over look
Before her I-succumb-to-your-overture sigh.

She is informing him, in so many words:
'There's more marmalade in the pantry';
'The hammer's in the drawer in the hall table';
'The washing machine needs a new drum'.

All art aspires to the condition of music.
My mother is a double-bass instrument whom
My father has played with passionate discretion.
Call it what you will - desire or affection -
Radiance or obscurity -
As couples go, their mutual attention to detail
I find very moving, not to say very uplifting.
For myself, I am my father without my father's shoulders
And a woman one eighth as genetic as my mother
Would benefit me down to the ground:
(singing)   *Down to the ground;*
              Down to the ground, down to the ground, down to the ground;
              Down to the ground.

Man With Two Daughters

I

My wife lives in another city
With - or without - another man;
Please God with another man.
We meet from time to time
To weigh our two daughters,
Adjust weights on the weighing scales.
She laughs, lighting up a cigarette.
'You have them looking like a pair of caged birds.'
I love her as I have always loved her.
We will never live together again.

My girls - do they look like caged birds?
'Beauty is the harmony of chance and the good.'

Such carriage, such poise
The little one has - she could be
Doge of Venice the way she holds herself.

Her older sister - so at ease
With the world, she stands in profile to it.

A pair of mallard ducks, vertical in canal water,
Tails-up, upended off the pebbled shore of the universe,
All bill, all eye.

The younger looks to the older
And the older looks to the world;
I look to the pair of them.

I have only to put my hands on their shoulders
To feel the hairs on the backs of my hands lie down;
To feel the peace percolate through my bones;
The medieval stream that flows beneath our home;
Our urbanity fluid between granite setts.

MAN WITH TWO DAUGHTERS
Giambattista Moroni

A sunsoaked afternoon in Brescia
With my daughters
Has a different definition of light
To a sunsoaked afternoon in Brescia
Without my daughters.
Everything I am
I owe to them;
My two infinitely gentle,
Infinitely suffering daughters.

II

We will attend to our father ourselves.
We will illuminate his nights and days
With gold skirts and orange skirts;
With the stuff of taffeta;
Green-and-white bodices;
Starched ruffs.
We will mantle him.
We will dismantle him.
He will dwindle down into a blade of grass
In a forest of silks.
We will not desert him.
We will smother him
In daughterdominion; sisterchaos; womancalm.

CAIN AND ABEL
Circle of Riminaldi circa 1620

28

Cain And Abel

My name is Cain MacCarthy.
I am a Senior Counsel, forty-nine years old.
A Bencher of the King's Inns.
No humbler fellow could you meet outside a courtroom.
Inside a courtroom I am pedigree ape.

When I get a witness in the witness box
I imbibe the witness's entrails
Only to spit them out again,
Draping them - entrail by entrail -
On the rails of the witness box.

I earn £700,000 a year before tax.
I do not deny they are entitled to tax me
But I protest at the exorbitant tax
That overworked barristers like myself have to pay
To subsidise blackguards like my brother.

My brother. Yes. My brother.
He is a priest. God help us.
Father Abel C.S.S.P..
To spell it out, a Holy Ghost.
Spent most of his life in South America.
Would to Jesus Christ he had stayed there.
Things were okeydoke so long as he was away on the missions
But every time he'd land home on leave
There'd be trouble. Nothing would do my wife
But to invite him to break bread with us
Every other night of the week - she could not have enough
Of him. I was sick of the pair of them
Nattering away about Social Justice and Liberation Theology,
Papal Encyclicals, *Rerum Novarum, Quadragesimo Anno,*
And - one of his party pieces - how the beggars in Nassau Street -
Those good-for-nothing tinker teenage mothers and their pups -
Are icons of the Holy Mother and the Infant Jesus
And, as if all that were not enough, Poetry!
Poetry! To behold her eyes gaping at him
As he quoted Oscar Wilde or some such alcoholic pansy
Was enough to make me puke my roast lamb.

It was the night he criticised my colleague Mr Wyse Power
- One of the most patriotic advocates ever to grace the bar -
That I flipped my lid. I grabbed him by the curlies
And dragged him out the French door into the back garden.
'Oh no! Oh no' - I could hear him moan.
But I was in a cocoon of my own.
My youngest kiddie's baseball bat was on the sill
Of the utility room and that is how I did it.
I beat him to death with a baseball bat and as I did it
I called to mind having intercourse with my wife
On our last holiday in Florida.
We have a time-sharing apartment in Orlando, Florida.

As I thumped him
I developed an erection
And I felt profoundly calm,
Profoundly humble.

My belovèd brother, I never knew you
Until this moment. I never knew
That deeper than my lechery for my wife
Was my detestation of you.
Although I married my wife for the broad view of her hips
And in terms of bed pleasure she has not let me down
- In fact, she'd jump over the moon
With me gripping onto her breasts
With my teeth if I told her to -
I have never known such pleasure
As I have known in the liquidation of my brother.
As he gasped his last gasp for mercy
I could feel my right nipple stiffen
In a lilac halo.
I switched on the t.v. and watched a half-hour of Gulf War.
When the police came I told them he had attacked me.
Naturally they believed me.

Interior With Figures

I go to meet my bridegroom
Whom I have never met before:
Over his arm, my overcoat.

In a corner of the chamber
My parents sit in silence.
A place is laid at table -
A place for him
If he can distil himself.

He says to me:
May I store my china in your buffet-gast?
I say to him:
You may.

INTERIOR WITH FIGURES
Nicolas de Gyselaer

ACIS AND GALATEA
Nicolas Poussin

Acis And Galatea

Not long after we became lovers, when she was appointed
Minister for the Environment there was a brouhaha -
First woman minister etc..
When the pandemonium had evaporated - is there anything
More ephemeral than newspaper news or more dispiriting? -
We continued as before stealing a couple of hours when we could
(From the cares of office in her case,
From the cares of no office in mine)
To take a stroll down the Bull Wall. Dublin is an exotic city,
More exotic than Naples which most sensually resembles it,
Its most exotic aspect being the Wild Life Sanctuary
Down the Bull Wall on the north shore of the Bay.

Many's the weekday afternoon we lay in the dunegrass
Having made love, and mused - gazing at the city up above us -
The marsh around us all lark, rabbit, goose,
The odd Nereid 500, the odd Triton 50 -
Can there be any other city in the world -
In South America or in Africa or in Australasia -
Where you can make love on the main street, so to speak,
And nobody notices? Except for the one-eyed columnist
Who carries small sharp stones in the pockets of his dinner jacket;
Polyphemus for whom malice is a melody;
Squeezing the last drop of bitterness from his wee flute.

Polyphemus slides past as Galatea sinks down her forefinger,
Its varnished nail, between my chin and my knee,
Swishing his red towel. A great man for his daily swim.
Never misses his daily swim. She's back in her office
Receiving delegations from Green Peace and Earth Watch
Before she has wholly shaken the sand out of her hair,
My imminent death by stoning never intimidating us.
Our Bull Wall days - Poussinimity!

THE VENERATION OF THE EUCHARIST
Jacob Jordaens

The Veneration Of The Eucharist

I

I am disappointed when after Mass
As we sit into your red Fiat,
Overloaded with Sunday newspapers,
You remark that at Holy Communion
You observed me standing in line
To receive the Eucharist.

As a vision of fact the Eucharist
Is all that matters to me.
Inarticulate with post-coital grief
If I could tell you - which I cannot -
I would tell you that every moonburst
We have intercourse, you and I,
It is a eucharistic union.
I place my two hands on your thighs,
Hold you up to our sea-strewn skies.

I am the cross you must gladly bear.
You are the cross I must gladly bear.
The children that may or may not
Be shed to us
Will live their lives with flaming hearts,
Will have crosses of their own to gladly bear.

II

I am standing at the counter of the newsagents
Feeling guilty for having bought *The Irish Times*
When I notice in the doorway a lion of mature years
With a young woman sitting sidesaddle
Whom I instantly recognise
But whose name I cannot remember.
She is holding up the Eucharist in a monstrance.
Her white dress is cut low - giving full rein
To the champagne ponies of her breasts,
A sturdy pair of Connemara ponies.
The lion growls, his glazed eyes glaring beyond me.

I shrink back against the counter
Ready to receive the Eucharist
But apprehensive of the lion; to leap into her bosom
And to die forever -
Not to die for a half-day or a day or a week
But to die forever.
The lion nudges me out of the way at the counter.
Chiding me for not remembering her name
She dispenses the host to me on the tip of my tongue:
The Body of Christ.
My hands joined, my eyes closed,
I exit out of the shop backwards.
That's all I have ever wanted to do - to die forever.

Kitchen Maid With The Supper At Emmaus

I

I am perched on the kitchen counter
Watching the kitchen maid at her art.
Having disposed of the washing up
She is drying and polishing.

I am swinging my legs, fancying her.

I envy her for being herself:
Each kitchen utensil for being itself;
Everything for being in relation to everything:
Each in its place, she in hers:
Servant of the servant of the Lord:
Oblivious of me fancying her.

KITCHEN MAID WITH THE SUPPER AT EMMAUS
Diego Velázquez de Silva

She is attending to vase and bowl:
Vase and bowl are attending to one another.
She has left the hatch open behind her.
Nosily I ask her: Who are the men in the hatch?
Slowly she spins around and closes the hatch.

There are three men in the hatch.
Three men striking a bargain.
One of them making a drawing sign.

I ask her: what sort of drawings does he do?
She says: if you want to know, he does drawings of sheep.

I continue in silence to swing my legs.
She says: you can see for yourself his sheep drawings
In the caves all around Emmaus.
She adds: I will show them to you, if you would like me to.

II

Even as I speak to you
Down the line from my kitchen
In Emmaus in County Mayo
The bowl which I have polished
Is lying up against the vase
Licking it and nuzzling it,
The pair of them lying up against
One another like a pair of cats
Jostling in a spot of sunlight.

Me? I am crouching,
Lying up against myself
With a jug in my hand, telling
What my eyes have already told me -
That the vase is dancing with the bowl.

I do not need eyes
In the back of my head
To know that when vases
Begin dancing with bowls
It is time to relax
My grip on the jug handle.

I have forgotten what it was
I was about to pour out of,
Or into, the jug.
But the jug also like myself
Is intending to say something:
That my jacket half-open at the navel
Will be the inlet of your desire.

I serve at the table of the Lord.

When I have put down the telephone,
Done speaking with you,
Returned the pestle to its mortar,
I will close the cupboard of the Lord,
Put back the key in the basket on the nail,
Spend the evening ironing his dresses.
I could go on forever ironing the dresses of the Lord.
I will go on forever ironing the dresses of the Lord.

SAINT CECILIA
Iacopo Vignali

Saint Cecilia

When I was a nineteen year old girl
They tried to turn me into a virgin
But I held onto my innocence
By becoming a mother
Of nineteen children -
One for every year of my life.
I am forty nine years old today
Celebrating my nineteenth birthday.

It has not been a cakewalk.
Female columnists threatened me with exposure
If I did not become a virgin.
They motored slowly around Ringsend after me,
A loudspeaker on their car roof rack:
'A Virgin Thou Wilt Be For Evermore'.

I hid from them in the restaurant
Of the National Gallery of Ireland.
A cup of coffee restored my spirits
After which, in the restoration department,
Sergio Benedetti restored my face
Until at last I became myself again
And I was fit to go back to my work -
Washing floors in public toilets:
An ideal job for when I was raising
My kids. When my poor martyr of a husband
Was not on the ran-tan he would mind house
While I was down slaving in the toilets.

My two sisters - a pair of angels -
One of them is a virtuoso lutanist -
She wears Michael Cullen wristwarmers
And Caravaggio epaulettes - both of them
Got my head loaded into politics and I was elected
To the corporation on the Singing Charlady Ticket
And the next thing I was elected Lord Singing Mayor,
Everyone calling me by my first name Cecilia.

I stood in the Euro elections as the Independent Singing Charlady.
Saint Cecilia for Europe. I added 'Saint' for euphony.
I was elected on the first count
With 78,000 first preference votes.
In the official European Parliament vade mecum
There is a passport photo of me with my c.v..
I am very proud of that, I have to tell you,
As are my nineteen kids,
Their poor martyred father dead and buried up in Mount Jerome,
God be good to him, he was always on the ran-tan.

At forty-nine my virginity is no longer a problem.
I can have any man I want
Without let or hindrance
Secure in the status of my musicality,
Not having to worry about any more pregnancies.
It was grand having the children
But nineteen is enough and I wouldn't mind
Not having had them and instead sung songs
But on the other hand you can sing while you're having them
Or have them while you're singing.
I am still basically the same girl I always was,
The same Dublin virgin with knobs on,
My tuning key always at the ready
On a white napkin on my red tablecloth -
An old altercloth the parish priest gave me.

I still walk to work every day
Except when I have to get a plane
To Brussels or S-bourg.
I will never buy a motor car as long as I live
No matter what which way
My local friendly Opel dealer chats me up.
It would be against all my musical principles
To purchase a motor car.

From harmony, from heavenly harmony
This universal frame began:
Sing up, girls:

    Blown glass;
    All I want in my window is blown glass.

    Tree rings;
    All I want in my elbow sleeve is tree rings.

    And -
    Beautiful cracking until the crack of dawn.

    Blown glass;
    Tree rings.

    When you climb into bed and it is very late at night
    Take off your panties and aim them at the chair;
    If they miss the chair, they will hit the floor;
    Keep your hair on, do not fret anymore -
    Beautiful cracking until the crack of dawn.

THE LEVITE AND HIS CONCUBINE AT GIBEAH
Jan Victors

The Levite And His Concubine At Gibeah

After Paul Durcan left his wife
- Actually she left him but it is more *recherché* to say
That he left her -
Would you believe it but he turned up at our villa
With a woman whom we had never heard of before,
Much less met. To *our* villa! The Kerrs of Dundalk!
I, Mrs Kerr, with a windowframe around my neck!
You will not believe it but he actually asked me
To put him up for the night - and his friend -
A slip of a thing, half his age.
I said that I would but in separate bedrooms.
This is a family home - I had to remind him.
I resented having to remind him.

The pair of them proceeded to squat in silence
In the living room for what was left of the evening
So that I could not even switch on the television.
As a consequence I missed 'Twin Peaks'.
What got up my nose
Was that she sat on the step of the fireplace
On a cushion from our sofa thrown down by him
With her hands joined around his knees:
Himself sitting in my husband's armchair
As if he owned it - without so much as a 'May I?'

She was got up in a loudspoken yellow dress
And those precious little hands of hers around his knees
As if his knees were pillows;
Her face a teatowel of holy innocence
As if margarine would not melt in her tonsils.
I would go so far as to say that it was indelicate -
The way she had her hands joined around his knees.

As soon as I began to yawn, he began to speak:
Holding forth until three o'clock in the a.m.
On what he called his 'Theory of Peripeteia' -
A dog's dinner of gibberish about the philosophical significance
Of 'not caring being the secret to transforming misfortune'.
Finally I stood up and declared 'Peripeteia, Goodnight'.
I installed the pair of them in separate bedrooms.
I left my own bedroom door open.

I fell asleep about five.
When I knocked him up for breakfast
She answered the door. I was that indignant
That when they came down for breakfast
I gave them porridge - like it or lump it.
I did not utter one word to them
Until they had finished.
Then I took him aside and I let him have it:

Now listen to me Paul Durcan:
You may be a poet and a Levite
But you will not take advantage of me.
Get yourself and your - your - your concubine
Out of my Dundalk villa.
How dare a woman wear a loudspoken yellow dress -
When you set foot in Gibeah next time
Do not ever Durcan my doorstep again.

Know what his response was? To ask me
If he might borrow my Shell Guide and my donkey?
To be rid of him I gave in - more fool I.
He shimmied out the door singing to himself:
'We borrowed the loan of Kerr's big ass
To go to Dundalk with butter ...'

Know what he did then? He went down to that old peasant
In the lane at the end of the avenue - Kavanagh -
Who goes about the town always with his socks down
Because he used play football for Mucker-Rotterdam:
Kavanagh with that - that ridiculous -
That - that vulgar -
That - that gross
Brass knocker on his front door.

THE SLEEPING SHEPHERDESS
Jan Baptist Weenix

The Sleeping Shepherdess

I

I am an attendant in the National Gallery.
I am not ashamed to say it -
One of the most assiduous attendants they have had
In the history of the National Gallery.
They call me 'The Sleeping Shepherdess'.
I tend to fall asleep from time to time.
I have my periods. We all do.
My flock of pictures know me.
My pictures and I have been together
For thirty odd years day in, day out.
Me gazing at them, them gazing at me.
No, they know. They do not climb down off the walls
And scarper - they take it in turns to attend me
Knowing as James White, that goodly shepherd, stated:
The most beautiful picture in the world is not worth one human life.

II

She sleeps. I bark. A matter of trust.
In her hat which upside-down is her husband's boat.
She picks me up in her two hands,
Holds me between her lead white breasts.

She smiles. I kick my legs.
I wet her lead white bosom with my wet snout.
I dig into her buttocks with my paws.
Her technique in affection as in sleep -
Improvised, measured, sweet, ferocious.

There is no mystery to compare
With the mystery of trust;
The mystery of a woman sleeping;
A woman sleeping in daylight.
The golden rule of the golden age:
Dogs do not talk in front of a woman sleeping.

THE RIDING SCHOOL
Karel Dujardin

The Riding School

Dung, cobble, wall, cypress;
Delight in art whose end is peace;
No cold-eyed horseman of the Irish skies
Can compare with me
Leading out the Grey of the Blues.

I in my red blanket
Under the Cave Hill Mountain
Leading out the Grey of the Blues:
The blindness of history in my eyes;
The blindness of history in my hands.

To get up at four every morning
And to lead out the Grey of the Blues;
Delight in art whose end is peace;
Hold his reins with my eyes open;
His dappled hindquarters;
His summer coat;
His knotted mane;
His combed-out tail;
His swanface;
His bullneck;
His spineline;
His tiny, prancing grace-notes.

And I in my red blanket
Under the Cave Hill Mountain
Leading out the Grey of the Blues:
The blindness of history in my eyes;
The blindness of history in my hands.

I take pride in my work;
Delight in art whose end is peace;
The way I lead out a song;
The way I hold the reins of a song in my hands
Between my stubby fingers.
I talk to my song;

My song talks to me.
In the blackest weathers
We have our sunniest hours.
How many early mornings
In black rain I have talked my song
Round and round the pink paddock!

I in my red blanket
Under the Cave Hill Mountain
Leading out the Grey of the Blues:
The blindness of history in my eyes;
The blindness of history in my hands.

My song is nearing the end of its tether;
Lament in art whose end is war;
Opera glasses, helicopters, t.v. crews;
Our slayings are what's news.
We are taking our curtain call,
Our last encore.
True to our natures
We do not look into the camera lenses
But at one another.
In a gap of oblivion, gone.

I in my red blanket
Under the Cave Hill Mountain
Leading out the Grey of the Blues:
The blindness of history in my eyes;
The blindness of history in my hands.

Lady Mary Wortley Montagu

I

At the American Roundabout in Constantinople
I was thrown from a fast-moving motorcar
By its driver Lady Mary Wortley Montagu -
A lovers' falling out with bread knives, broken bottles, nail scissors.

II

I worked for her.
I was her clavicytherium.
Oh yes her clavicytherium.
For four years.

My role each evening
To stand nude in the bay window
Overlooking the Gates of Horn;
She in white satin gown,
Blue three-quarter length coat,
Standing beneath me,
Tickling my keys.

When I'd bleat in that sheepish tone
Unique to lovers
'Do you need me Mary?'
She'd nod her jowls and growl
'You are the feather in my cap'
And she'd coax my clavichords
With her white turban's long black feather.

When I'd query her
'Am I your - your indispensable gnome?'
She'd moan into my flaring nostril
'Dearest - I could not play a note without you.
Why - you are my metronome.'

LADY MARY WORTLEY MONTAGU
Charles Jervas

54

She'd start to pluck and tickle, tickle and pluck
Until astringently she'd cease
And I'd disintegrate onto the floor
In a soup of harpstrings.

As I trickled about on the Turkey carpet
Clutching its fringes
She'd make a show of ankle:
'I'm wearing the cherry-red tights
You bought me at Troy.'
She'd step out of her underwear,
All mind over matter,
Pick me up in her arms
And whisk me into her bathroom -
A converted drawing-room with lavatory and bidet
At one end and at the far end the shower.

My last task of the day -
To swing out of the shower head
While she had a shower:
'One's bathroom should be like a long poem'
She'd roar, anticipating Keats,
'A place to wander in.'
She was always anticipating Keats.

III

O Montagu
How can I not say it
You caribou you -
You eighteenth century London caribou you -
I had a dose of you.

I read in the back page of the *Sunday Independent*
That she has gone to live in Natal
With a mountain lion, stroking his tail
And reading aloud to him. In the long African tights
- I mean in the long African nights -
He sits on her, smoking his pipe
And she likes that - the long African nights.

THE DILETTANTI

Cornelius Troost

The Dilettanti

My boy is playing a lullaby
But I am not at all certain
Who his mother is.
Difficult to sit still and concentrate.
My feeling is that his mother
Was a Haarlem cleaning woman
Who drowned herself in a canal
The Michaelmas before last.

I fancy Susanna was her name.
I think so because when he began to play
I observed the corner of the carpet sit up
And make faces at me and display
A particular charlady's prominent front teeth
Cascading forth her red-blue lips, O God.
I am drumming my fingers,
My paunch in dry dock.

Bishop Robert Clayton
And His Wife Katherine

I

My dear children of God, - I am an old cod
But once I was a young cod on the Grand Tour
Delighting and delighted. I held forth on sport
And war, quoting *ad nauseam* from the classics;
Tibullus, Virgil, Archilochos, Propertius.
'He eats, drinks, and sleeps in taste' -
Lord Orrery wrote of me. He did!
I say to you: I, your bishop, incite matrimony
In spite of all the inconvenience it entails.
Which is why you behold me in my portrait gaze
Not upon myself nor upon a *mememto mori*
Nor upon any other specious bauble of *vanitas*
But upon my wife Katherine in her unique chair
With its splat in the shape of a love-heart;
Upon her decolletage
In whose umbrageous rocks divinity dwells,
Dwells the godhead.

I ponder not upon her educated and cultivated mind
- A Donnellan to her knees, I can tell you -
But upon her carnal fault which is her soul.
I hold with Catullus and with Sappho and with Christ.
I hold with intuition of the votive earth
From which I come, to which I will return,
The votive earth which alone adorns my sleeve.
I hold the Gospel in my left hand.
Her thigh in my right hand.
Although First Love can never be repeated
I live in faith that she may yet again
Row out my little boat upon her lough.

BISHOP ROBERT CLAYTON AND HIS WIFE KATHERINE
James Latham

II

This Xmas morning on our way across to church,
A gravel path of not more than fifty yards
From scullery to sacristy,
Between herbaceous borders,
We succumbed, my dear wife and I, to grimacing
In a sort of embroidery at one another.

III

This Xmas night
I having placed three pillows beneath her back
She will draw back her knees up past her cheeks
Until her knees recline upon her shoulders
So that I can douse her haunches with my tongue,
Install myself inside her,
Until we two are become as one divinity;
One divinity crouched in interlocking stillness on a bough;
The sole sound - the small rowboat of my member
Bobbing on the waters of her lough.
In the Name of the Father, and of the Son, and of the Holy Ghost.
Amen.

JOSEPH LEESON
Pompeo Batoni

Joseph Leeson

I am a chap
Who dictates his best novels
Standing at the urinal.

Indeed, it ought to be clear from Batoni's portrait of me
(A beauty of a chap himself - Batoni)
That I am a chap of the first water.

In twenty-seven words:
The sort of chap who even while he waits
His turn to go the gents
In his mother's fur hat
Holds himself in
With verisimilitude, tact, ego.

AN INTERIOR WITH MEMBERS OF A FAMILY
Philip Hussey

An Interior With Members Of A Family

Sir, Mam, we are agreed
That in family portraiture
Families are incidental
To fixtures and fittings.

In our portrait, therefore, precedence
Accrues to the keyhole fireplace,
To the pole-screens,
To the architectural wall paper,
To the sixteen dining chairs
As many of which we will slip in
As we may. You, Sir, will account
For one chair by leaning on one chair
Truantly with tincture of propriety.

Pride of place perforce goes
To the carpet which I will deploy
Tilting inwards, exhaling sensation
Of being about to devour entire family
Than which, Sir, Mam, advertisement
No grander can I devise for you.

The family of today
Is the family that gets carried away
By its own carpet.

The Earl Of Bellamont

I like a man who does not care.
The Earl of Bellamont arrives into the National Gallery
Every other day for luncheon in the restaurant
But he does not merely arrive in - he splashes down,
Unbattening the hatches as he splashes,
Firing off kisses to all and sundry,
To non-entities as well as entities.
The Earl of Bellamont is a man who does not care.

The get-up, the get-out of him.
Created by Sir Sploshua.
He does a line in cloaks and today
It is a pink flesh-toned affair
Noosed at the breast with two lengths of cord
From whose terminals dangle between his thighs
A pair of tassels -
A pair of the most affable, episcopal, ding-dong, sedate,
     steadfastest, one-eyed
Tassels.
The Earl of Bellamont is a man who does not care.

He takes his place in the queue in the restaurant.
While waiting for his lasagne to hot up in the microwave
He leans nonchalantly on his swordstick
Airing his opinions on the state of the art market:
'Every man should apprise himself of his own value.
I cost £550 - that is exactly to the penny
What Henry Doyle paid for me.
You see before you £550 worth of pure Coote.'
As he airs he slowly crosses his legs
To give ample recognition not only to his tassles
But to his rosettes:
On each suede slipper a pink rosette.
'Tassels are all' he complains
'And yet rosettes are more.'
The Earl of Bellamont is a man who does not care.

THE EARL OF BELLAMONT
Joshua Reynolds

Like all regulars in the National Gallery Restaurant
He has his favourite pew and woe betide
You who would purloin it from him - you will be woebegone.
It is the table adjacent to Power's *Fish*.
He keeps his hat on in deference to Power's *Fish*.
When foreign visitors focus their attention
What they behold is a green fish soaring up some marble
In a grove of white feather and plume
While on his lap he cradles his tassels.
Not like others I have seen in the National Gallery
Cradling objects more obnoxious than any tassel -
Be it a tassel of a Coote or a Bulfin.
The Earl of Bellamont is a man who does not care.

After luncheon in the National Gallery Restaurant
We diverge outside at the statue of Shaw:
I to Sybil in the Rutland Memorial Fountain
In drizzle rejoicing in life, literature and art;
He to his tubes in Trinity College
To which he owns a postern gate key.
I have never asked him what exactly
His work is - but I gather
It is in software, not surprisingly.
The Earl of Bellamont is a man who does not care.

MRS CONGREVE WITH HER CHILDREN
Philip Reinagle

Mrs Congreve With Her Children

Although I am the girl's mother
I have to admit I fear for the lives of her men
When she is a grown gal.

Many is the garden path,
The exotic shrub, she will lead them up
With that squirrel of hers.

Even if ever they catch hold of her squirrel
It will either slip out of their hands
Or nip them in the wrists.

That squirrel of hers will eat a buck's nuts
Until a buck's got no nuts left -
London town littered with bucks with no nuts.

My little boy with his cannon is the soul of predictability
Like my husband up the wall behind me. He will be a proper husband.
Good, dull, fire off his cannon at regular intervals.

My other daughter is a worm - a bookworm.
I see no future for her unless she learns to ride a horse
And marries a farmer.

Most likely she will marry a divorced antiquarian
And become his devoted and unhappy wife, silly girl.
I do not really pity her one farthing.

She does not know anything. Thinks this drawing room fell out of the sky
Would not know a carver from a girandole or a hand-knotted pile
Or whether her ancestor's portrait was a Kit-Cat or not.

She does not know her carpets - Axminister, Turkish,
Transylvanian, Smyrna, Sparta piles - all the same to her.
What hope is there for a gal who does not know her carpets?

BISHOP OF DERRY WITH HIS GRANDDAUGHTER
Hugh Douglas Hamilton

Bishop Of Derry With His Granddaughter

Life in all its glory is booty for the Bold

When I sit in my palace
In Finglas
And contemplate my lion's foot,
Calculate what it signifies,
What it metaphysically signifies
To be a bishop
- The awesome obligations
Of a bishopric -
I appreciate why bishops
Arc so gallantly fond
Of small girls,
So ostentatiously fond
Of small girls.

Discretion, however,
Is called for.
I do not think it appropriate
For a Bishop of God
To commission a portrait
Of himself with a small girl
Particularly when - as in Derry's case -
The small girl is positioned
At the centre of the panorama
While the bishop is relegated
To one side or the other,
The impression thereby conveyed
That a small girl has precedence
Over a Bishop of God.

Confessedly however - in Derry's case -
The Bishop has adopted a humble
And virginal pose
And I think that his joined hands,
His jovially joined hands,
Which mirror his crossed legs,
His jovially crossed legs,
Betokeneth humility and concord.

With due respect to my brother bishops
I do not think I have ever seen
In an episcopal prelate
Such delicacy of knee,
Such magnanimity of foot,
Such piety of fingerjoints
And I know what he is thinking,
Alas I do. He is thinking -

For many is the occasion I myself
Have taken a small girl to the cinema
And been emancipated by those credulous eyes
Forever gazing upward into the silver screen.
While she watches the images flicker
I am consoled to observe her -
To observe the motion picture of her innocence.
There is nothing so enthralling to a bishop
As he sits - or stands - puce in his blacks -
As the picture of innocence in motion.

He is thinking that in a few years
She will be no longer a small girl
And who knows what the future
Will bring - not even a bishop
Except, of course, a bishop with capital.
One thing that re-assures me
When I am taking out small girls
Is the recollection that I never touch
My capital. I live always
On my income most of which I re-invest
In *objets d'art*. I have amassed so many *objets d'art*
I am obliged to amass much of it under my bed.

When I am tucked up at night
After my saucer of cocoa
(Never a cup - always a saucer -
A bishop must always show example,
A bishop must always stay true to his rural roots)
Under my electric blanket
Gazing out upon the homeless under the stars,
God's chosen people of homelessness under the stars
And at the lonely masses on their lonely planets
It helps me to go to sleep to count
All the small girls I have ever known
And, simultaneously, my money;
To recollect that I live solely on my income.
I blow smoke rings into the dark.
Cheroots, not cigarettes, are the thing.
I never touch my capital.

Bishops are such seminal, rational men.
Which is why, I surmise, God chooses them.

SIR JOHN AND LADY CLERK OF PENICUIK
Henry Raeburn

Sir John And Lady Clerk Of Penicuik
With Fish

I

On the bus into town to Foreman's camera centre
- The number 3 bus from Ringsend to Westland Row -
I fret as to whether the snaps will come out;
The snaps of my mother with my two daughters;
She is seventy-five and they are in their twenties.

Soon as I disembark at Westland Row
I discover that I have lost the roll of film.
Leaving the house in a panic this morning
I forgot to pull over the zip of my shoulder bag.

I slip into Westland Row church,
Kneel half-way down the empty nave.
When pieces of life's jigsaw are found
We are born but when they are lost
I am no longer my mother's son,
My daughters are somebody else's daughters.

Into the holy water font in the porch
I dip my hand but there is no water - stone
For a fish to expire in. With air
I scribble the sign of the cross - my forefinger flitting
Across my forehead, my breast, my shoulders.

No Bicycles - writ not on water
But on the palings in front of the church.

I will take my life in my hands:
My impaled bicycle,
My lost roll of film.
I will walk up Westland Row.
I will walk past Oscar Wilde's birthplace.
I will walk past the Royal Irish Academy of Music.
I will nearly get knocked down at the traffic lights.
I will rejoice outside Sweny's Druggists.

I will go into the National Gallery Restaurant.
I will have a coffee and think things over,
See if the balance of the picture can be restored,
Balance weight against weightlessness.
I sit down beside Power's *Fish*.

In all my years of sitting beside Power's *Fish*
I have not noticed until this morning
That he gouged in the marble *1944* -
The year of my birth.
His fish is swimming in stone -
A creature down on his hands and knees
Snapping his mother and daughters.

Thinking things over, I think of 'Hamlet' -
The Russian poem by Pasternak taught me
By my younger daughter and of the woman
I met last night on the last number 3 bus -
The very picture of Ophelia,
Such laughter, such tears, such lipstick -
Who blurted out of the blue if I would mind
If she asked me a question. 'Not at all' I said.
She blushed and stopped speaking. I had to tell her
That by 'Not at all' I meant 'Yes'.
She said: 'Do you believe in Fate or Chance?'
In both - I replied
Wondering immediately after I had spoken if I had lied.

'100,000 casualties in one day' -
It was stated on 'Morning Ireland' this morning.
100,000 acts of love;
100,000 acts of war.
100,000 pangs;
100,000 throes.

To live your life is not as easy
As to cross a field or to be a fish in water.
To live your life is to lose your film of it
And having lost it to go on swimming in stone.
While I am thinking it over, thinking of Ophelia,
A visitor to the gallery hangs his hat on Power's *Fish*
And sits down with his back to it, talking in a low voice
About Raeburn's *Sir John and Lady Clerk of Penicuik.*
The visitor whispers to his wife: 'Raeburn's a *rara avis*'.

As I talk to you, Ophelia,
You are a fish
Whom God having caught
God loses or throws
Back into the sea.
To live your life is as difficult
As to be a fish in stone
With somebody else's hat on your head.

II

I stand up and keeping my arms folded
I skate out of the restaurant
And skim the parquet to the Scottish corner:
Raeburn's *Sir John and Lady Clerk of Penicuik;*
His cuffs in a white heat to meet
The little black bow of her enamel bracelet;
His forefinger proposing ecstasy -
Weightlessness
To her weight.

FISH
Albert Power

'By the hokey, Rosemary,
Trust you to take the air
In your white nightgown - straight
After having your shower - well
Here it is, the old place -
Your new home for evermore.
What do you make of it?
D'ye agree that these wee bare moors
In their lofty scantiness
Are more than a wee bit romantic?
Do not be shy, my love,
You were not last night.
My luminous, transparent Rose
My ferocity with our romance grows.
Why the puzzlement on your brow?
Thou ratherest thy bed I know
But it is five after twelve I vow
And I to Edinburgh must go
To meet with Raeburn.
No, not the doctor Raeburn - the limner Raeburn.

Dear love, how rumpled-glad you look.
I know we're middle-aged but still -
There's a limit to the rumpled-gladness
In a woman's complexion a lad can endure
At five after twelve in the afternoon.
There's aye not enough grey in thy hair.
Still thou art ravishing, my Rose.
If thou don's't go indoors this instant
I will have you beneath this very tree
In my hat, cravat, jacket, breeches and all,
This very beech my grandsire planted.
You'd like that? In earnest?
Don't you ever feel the cold, Rosemary?
Alright, this once, being the day after our wedding day.
But for the future I forbid my wife to wander
Our estate in scanty night attire.

Well, then, to it Rose, undo me.
By Harry you may enjoy me
As I intend wholly to enjoy thee.
To think - to think, my earthy Rose,
That exactly two hundred years from today
In the collection of the National Gallery of Ireland -
You and I being caught in the act
In flagrante delicto
Beneath the old tree at Penicuik -
That we will constitute 'a key Raeburn'!
Hah! Don't tickle there! Here! Here!
Let's take aye a shower together.'

III

To celebrate - and to recover from -
Raeburn's Tribute to the Luck of Love
I walk through snow and sleet
To Bewley's Oriental Café
For a mug of white coffee.
Crowds sheltering from storms.
I get a seat by the open fire
In the Russian Chandelier Room.
The woman opposite me is a Scots woman.
From her conversation with the waitress
I can tell she is Edinburgh.
I can feel her eyes on me
And the coal fire at my back.
She is not the same woman
I met last night on the last bus
But she is very like her, Ophelia.
She does not greet me.
She does not speak to me
Of fate or chance.
She is reading a paperback
Entitled 'Sexual Power'.

I resolve not to inquire,
Not to intrude
Upon her anorexic moorland beauty.
When I rise to go, I say:
'Be seeing you'.
She whispers: 'Be seeing you'.
I walk to Foreman's camera centre
Only remembering when I get there
I have lost my roll of film.
I stand back out on the street,
A fish out of stone.
I put my two arms around a lamp-post,
Lean my frame up tight against it,
Hoping somebody will steal my wheels.
O my curly-headed Rose,
By 'Not at all' I mean 'Yes'.

Thomas Moore In His Study
At Sloperton Cottage

I

A writer is a worm;
Upon itself turns the screw
In clay cells of its own bastilles;
Voluntary incarceration.

'A prima donna of the carceral life' -
Is how our leading novelist puts it.

A creature whom you will find
On the sunniest, snowiest day of the year
Not gambolling about the laden meadows
With the other creatures of the wood -
The soft pink girls in their long black overcoats,
The squirrel, the fox, the hare, the hedgehog -
But down in the nightshade of his donjon
Scribbling by the light of the basement area;
Down in the dungeon of his own ribcage
Scribbling by the light of his own throat;
Down the tubes of his own larynx
Scribbling by the light of his own fear.

II

To be a writer
Is to be buried
Alive, first thing
Every morning.

I emerge from my bunker
At noon holding my head
Having written
Or as likely
Having not written
'Lalla Rookh'.

Carrying in my hand a poker
Thinking that it is not a harp
I stand blinking in daylight
Trying to remember
Who the blazes I am,
Where the blazes I am going,
What the blazes I am doing with a poker in my hand
Which I know very well is not a harp.
I am a very doughty, very glowing, very colic little Irishman
Held-up in rush-hour traffic in East Ham.

THOMAS MOORE IN HIS STUDY AT SLOPERTON COTTAGE
English School (19th century)

BATHERS SURPRISED
William Mulready

Bathers Surprised

Having been a bather in the foreground for many years
I would welcome leeway to tell my side of the story -
That I am not surprised at being surprised.
I have been waiting a long time to be surprised.
I was beginning to think I would never be surprised.
I can only hope that the next folio of my life
Will live up to my expectations. I am much afraid
That it will not. Bodies being bodies.

It should be tea-cosy pleasurable
But I have my doubts. Probably what will happen
Is that I will be impregnated.
That will mean matrimony which is not something,
If you have been a bather in the foreground,
You could ever vocationally desire for yourself
And after matrimony more impregnation,
Impregnation after impregnation
Until I am too old for impregnation anymore.

I will be a consummately good mother to my children
But that is not to say I would not have rathered a life
Not having children. Heresy. But true.
Truth is everything
To a bather in the foreground.
If only the ones who do the surprising
Could themselves be truthful.
But when it comes to balancing the accounts
Of their inner and their outer selves
Men diddle the books.

I will never be given leeway to tell my side of the story.
From being a bather in the foreground
A woman
Becomes a bather in the background
Waving for help;
Up to my knickers in water,
An old bra gesticulating from a rock.

DEMOSTHENES ON THE SEASHORE
Eugène Delacroix

Demosthenes On The Seashore

Have you ever encountered a man in Ireland
Whose mouth is not awash with pebbles?
Who is not most himself when attired
In scarlet pyjamas and buff dressing gown
Striding out the seashore to the corner store
To deliver his message to the grocer -
His ultimatum to mankind?

MARGUERITE IN CHURCH

James Tissot

Marguerite In Church

A franc for them?

The choice is: do I want to rise from the dead?
To live in sin with the right man, Dr Life,
Or to live in virtue with the wrong man, Dr Death?

I will marry Jesus
In spite of the fact that he is an atheist,
That he is twice my age,
That he is dead,
That he is a non-smoker,
That he is a non-drinker,
That he is the father of children,
That he has enemies,
That he is a poet,
That he is insomniac,
That he is half-bald, shortsighted, jowly,
Congealed in candlegrease.

I will marry Jesus
For his intelligence, his wit, his grace, his awkwardness;
For his extraordinary good sense, creative imagination, originality;
For his shyness, his fear, his audacity, his affection;
For his cniptiousness;
For his casual approach to everything;
For his informal ways which have many forms;
For his not being fussy about what clothes he wears
Nor about what time he gets up in the mornings.

In the long evening of my young life
He will tell me stories while I curl up at his feet
With my arms around his knees;
For him, alone, always, I will wear red and black.

The Meeting On The Turret Stairs

I

The meeting on the turret stairs
Is always musically the same;
The same turret, the same stairs;
The same streetcorner, the same lane;
The same treads, the same raisers;
The same noises, the same silences;
The same loop, the same sill;
The same stones, the same spotlights;
The same necessity to watch your step;
The same clinging, the same clasping;
The same nibbling of the other's shoulder;
The same shut eyes, the same rose petals;
The same turning away from one another;
The same circulation, the same percolation;
The same plaits; the same curls;
The same neck, the same torso;
The same girdle, the same sneakers;
The same nappy pins, the same vents;
The same lad, the same dame;
The same diminuendo, the same cascando.

She goes to her bedroom in the turret;
He goes to his motorbike in the basement
Where her brothers are waiting for him
To present him with an ultimatum;
Either you leave our sister alone
Or we will leave you alone
On Utopia Parkway - your lithe and limber torso
On one side of the highway - your helmeted skull
Galloping down the culvert on the other side.
Either way you must pay
For having dared to run away
With our sister to El Lay.

THE MEETING ON THE TURRET STAIRS
Frederic William Burton

II

Who would want it any other way?
It is only from the pain of our passing
That we derive our pleasure;
Lads passing one another in 'Books Upstairs',
On the turret stairs in 'Books Upstairs'
Overlooking Dame Street,
An ear out for the traffic far below;
The traffic in whose demise
The pennies are laid on our own eyes.

A GROUP OF CAVALRY IN THE SNOW
Ernest Meissonier

A Group Of Cavalry In The Snow

I

I crave snow.
I ride up to the National Gallery,
Make tracks for the narrow bluff
37.5 centimetres by 47 centimetres
By Jean-Louis Ernest Meissonier
'A Group Of Cavalry In The Snow'
Into which I can plunge my wrists.

I make snowballs in the gallery.
I go downstairs to the toilets,
Lob snowballs into the mirror
Until my fiery face is quite
Swathèd in snowflake;
Until my reflection in the mirror
Is quite swathèd in snowflake.

I am under-the-bed lonely friend
Like your polished boot;
Like your cloak by-gales-emptied-of-you strewn in snow.

II

My lover - most affectionate of creatures -
Tells me she no longer finds me bed company.

And you ask me why I look so disorientated?
Why are there hoofmarks in my face?

BOY EATING CHERRIES

Pierre Bonnard

Boy Eating Cherries

What Granny likes
Is to see a little boy eat up his cherries;
Little boys who eat up their cherries
Become big boys who eat up their cherries.

A MAN SEATED ON A SOFA
Edouard Vuillard

A Man Seated On A Sofa

In a coma on the sofa
With my back to the mirror;
If I had known then what now I know.

Mother and sister by the fireside;
I thinking that I am bored;
Searching for a pretext to exit -

To booze in a zinc bar with men
Instead of remaining in with my women,
Rejoicing in the mice behind the wainscotting -

Same as the rain
Scratching against the windowpane
And being in bed nipping champagne.

If I had known then what now I know
I'd have dived into the floorboards,
Sat out the afternoon as for a lifetime

In a coma on the sofa
Astonishing myself and being astonished
By the boney colatura of my women.

My fierce fragile mother, my fierce fragile sister,
Fireplace aslant from mantlepiece,
Knitting pullovers for nephews and nieces.

Two angelic cronies at my side,
Rocky paradise at my toes,
And I did not know it!

To be sitting out on the edge
Of things in the interior life,
Tangenital to genocide.

The Knucklebone Player

Two years after Paul died
I met Nuala cycling in the park
With Saturday's *Irish Times*
In her front wheel basket.
We fell to chatting about Paul:
What a cheerful, solitary fellow he was.
I asked her if there was anything of his
She would like as a souvenir,
Keepsake, relic.
After all - in the middle of all -
He had been her partner.
She whistled, nostalgically.

She said: I would like his knucklebones.
Both knucklebones?
Both knucklebones.
I promised her that the next time
The grave was opened
I would keep an eye out for Paul's knucklebones.

His father's death gave me the opportunity
To sift the soil for Paul's knucklebones.
One evening's sifting in late Spring
Threw up both knucklebones.
I sealed them in a jiffy bag,
A cassette-sized jiffy bag;
Dropped them through Nuala's letterbox.

Down the Hole-in-the-Wall
Midsummer's day
Strolling past the sunworshippers
I came upon Nuala topless
And poised, sitting up in the sand
Playing with something in her right hand,
Her left foot in her left hand,
Her hair tied up in a bun.

THE KNUCKLEBONE PLAYER

Gustav Natorp

In a slow, low voice -
Reminiscent of the phonograph recording
Of Oscar Wilde's rendition
Of 'The Ballad of Reading Gaol' -
She called me over:
'Each woman kills
The man she loves'.

Obscurely I could see
That what she was rattling
In the palm of her hand
Were Paul's knucklebones.
She was playing dice
With Paul's knucklebones.

Demurely she giggled: I have a friend -
A wood carver, a previous lover.
I commissioned him to make dice
Out of Paul's knucklebones:
'A throw of the dice
Never abolishes chance.'

I accepted her invitation
To share her lunch,
To play dice with her.
Sitting opposite her on her towel,
A lettuce leaf between my teeth,
I stared - she swallowed my stare whole -
Into her eyes prancing up and down
The small fences of her breasts,
Her eager never-pass-a-man eyes.

I said: Nuala -
You are a born knucklebone player.
She whistled: I am -
I am a born knucklebone player.

DAWN, CONNEMARA
Paul Henry

Dawn, Connemara

Black days
Are never so black as grey days.

See in the sky a face
Appearing pinkly over peaks,
Thin-lipped,
Bow-tied.

Pearse
Who left home.

He was different.
A degree in political science
Behind him.

He went to live in Mesopotamia
Where he spent fifteen years
Composing a poem about water,
Its origins and sources.

He died in Mesopotamia
In the war
During the Allied Bombing.

No one knows where his grave is -
If he ever had a grave.
Bone on the wind.

Pearse
Pinkly over peak.

In the office of the Taoiseach of Ireland
There is a small pewter jug on the mantlepiece:
Water of the River Euphrates
From his old school pal Pearse
Brought home in the diplomatic bag.

Supper Time

I

Riverside Drive.

Time passing, time passing timeless.
I am twenty-nine. Only yesteryear I was fourteen.
Cycling round the city libraries
Loading up my carrier basket with histories of art.

Loneliness passing, loneliness passing more
And more and more and illuminating -
Throwing light in detail
On what has been concealed for too long;
On the walnut table with the tablecloth
Rolled back for the visitor who will never come;
Reflection of the sugarbowl, the teapot and the fruitcake.

By my own hand. In my own studio. In my own time.

II

During the week my loneliness is dormant.
Only when I sit down at my married sister's table
Does my loneliness take on eyes and brows and hands and knees.

They conduct their supper time liturgy
As if I am not here;
I am in the La Scala cinema with the house lights on
Watching a wife celebrating Mass with her husband.

The husband is a great soldier, a great storyteller.
While he says the Gospel
My nephew is enchanted
As much by his father's nostrils as by his father's words;
My sister is about to say the words of the Consecration
As she pours milk from a silver jug:
'Do this in commemoration of me.'
My niece is colouring limbo in her colouring book.

SUPPER TIME

Patrick Tuohy

After the Consecration my sister folds her arms
Under her bosom and announces: Let us give thanks.

After Holy Communion - fruitcake and tea -
I feel secure in my loneliness.
My loneliness is my most precious gift.
To loneliness I owe all that I am.
Loneliness it is who gives me wings to cycle.
Loneliness has given me sovereignty over my body.

As I sit at my empty place at the table
The family is secure in its affection ;
Each member is a seed-vessel of affection.
The wallpaper as always is a steady shower.
Only rarely does it become a downpour.
Frequently it dwindles to a drizzle.

O my belovèd nephew and niece
To whom I hand sovereigns as I depart
One night you will spin around in your chairs
To behold a face at the window.
May that face not be my face
But I fear that it will.

By my own hand. In my own studio. In my own time.

Riverside Drive.

SELF-PORTRAIT IN THE ARTIST'S STUDIO
Moyra Barry

Self-Portrait In The Artist's Studio

Je sais. Je sais. Je sais.

Like all Irish women of my generation
Who resolved to seed themselves
I had to scatter to South America.

In the early years of the twentieth century
I, a genteel Dublin woman in my twenties,
Scattered to Quito in Ecuador
To teach art. My pupils taught me.

Taught by Ecuadorean Indians
That the human head is the primary seed-vessel.

So it was that when I,
A Dublin woman in Ecuador in 1920,
Sat to myself
To perform the ritual of the self-portrait,
Calling to mind Vincent in Provence,
I performed it as a chanson to my studio
- Itself a seed-vessel in passage across the seas -
But also as a chanson to my head,
Not evading my cowlike eyes, my rosebud mouth,
Plucking the fragility of my skull.

Father, what you must do
Is to cup my skull in your hands,
In your three hands,
And drink from it,
Drink from my skull
Until you have drunk me
To the dregs
Of my cerebral juices.
You will know,
Consumed by my grief,
By my humour,
The angostura bitters of daughterdom.

MAN WALKING THE STAIRS
Chaim Soutine

Man Walking The Stairs

Odd to overhear that you think I am saying
'Man walking the stars'
When all my life I have been saying
'Man walking the stairs'.

Living alone in a semi-detached villa
Between the mountains and the sea
I spend a great deal of time on the stairs.
Half way up the stairs
I pause at the window overlooking
The entrance to our cul-de-sac,
The lancet in my gable;
I pause for an hour or climb on.

When I get to the top of the stairs
I cannot remember why in the first place
I came up the stairs
But that is in the nature of living alone:
I am neither perplexed nor perturbed.
I go back downstairs and start
All over again, read another page,
Drink another cup of tea, hover
At the kitchen window, hover
At the front window, hover
In the hallway, hover
At the letterbox, hover
Before the looking glass in the coat rack
That we bought in Christy Bird's for two-and-sixpence.

I know what it is I must do.
I must go back upstairs and search
Under my bed for that book I have mislaid -
'The Oxford Dictionary of Quotations'.
I am searching for a line from Donne:
'Make my dark poem light'.
But I pause again at the gable window
This time to behold pine trees
Clutching at one another in a gale,
Pair of pines reprieved by the developer.

When I conquer the top of the stairs
I fall down the stairs,
All the way down to the foot of the stairs.
Lying at the foot of the stairs
For three days and three nights
I behold bills - gas bills
And telephone bills - Final Notices -
Swirl through the lips of the letterbox
And the attic trapdoor at the top of the stairs
Is flying, descending, circling, advancing.
It keeps getting closer to my face.
If they ever find me and I am still alive
They will accuse me of having been drinking,
Of having been at the sherry.
What is wrong with being at the sherry?
Pale dry sherry - her throat, her lips, her eyes.

I could never understand people
At any time but especially people
Advising me I ought to sell my home
Because of the stairs. 'What you must do
Is to find yourself a convenient bungalow
And save yourself the stairs.'
Like telling a man to swim in a pool with no water.
The whole point of my home
Is the stairs. Can you conceive
Of a life without stairs?

My life is the saga of a life on stairs.

When I was nine with my cousin William
Sliding down bannister rails
To crashland on beaches of linoleum
My father peering over cliffs down stairwells
Already unbuckling his trousers belt.

From thirteen to seventeen years
I sat on the stairs keeping vigil
With myself and the stair rods
Watching through bannister uprights
My father and mother coming and going.
I could not speak to them
Because when I spoke I stammered.
I clung to the bannisters,
Creature of the stairs.

Marriage at twenty-three and seventeen years
Of hoovering the stairs;
A flight of stairs and a hoover
And I was the sainted spouse.
Upstairs mowing away, I could hear
My wife downstairs whistling away
Scanning the morning paper.

Stairs into stairs.

One stair at a time or
Three stairs at a time or
Four or five stairs at a time
In our forties when she and I
Were to our bedroom racing
In the middle of the day
Barely able to reach it in time,
Slipping, clambering, getting there,
Her arms around my knees,
Or to the bathroom to bathe
Together in the same bath and make
A mess of water on the floor;
A pot of phlox on the window sill
Or a cruet of lambs tails from the hazel tree.

Days when we were not speaking
Or, truth to tell, days when
I was sulking and she kept out
Of my way, I'd sit all day
On the stairs, my knees tucked up
Under my chin, my elbows
Around my shinbones. I preferred
Sitting on stairs to sitting on chairs,
Sitting on the stairs facing the front door,
Facing south, facing south to the sea,
Remembering the Café Neptune in Batumi.

Man is the inventor of stairs.

How many miles of stairs
Have we walked together?
A great many, yet much less
Than the thousands of miles of stairs
I have walked alone.
I like to look around me on these long
Walks on the stairs;
Redwoods convulsed in gales, scots pines,
Olive trees, sycamores, my wife's ashes.

Man walking the stairs.
Man doing nothing else
Except walking the stairs.
Man scattering his wife's ashes
Either side of the stairs.
Sower stalking the stairs.

Our only son lived a long
And good life, only to be
Knocked down by a motor car
On Leeson Street Bridge.
We buried him in the front garden
Along with our two black cats.
I think of him on the stairs -
How he used crawl faceforwards
Down the stairs if I promised
To catch him at the foot of the stairs.

I carry my stairs in my arms
Up through the tree-tops of Provence,
All my treads and all my raisers.
Love is not love that is not courtly;
That's what every woman knows.

Man walking the stairs
Is man treading water.
Our house of water:
Do not open the door.

Odd to overhear that you think I am saying
'Man walking the stars'
When all my life I have been saying
'Man walking the stairs'.

A PORTRAIT OF THE ARTIST'S WIFE
William Leech

A Portrait Of The Artist's Wife
/A Self-Portrait

My sweetest wife
Although pain is our sole portion
I do thee honour.

I can no more disown you in your melancholy
Than I can disown you in your sleep.

But should your melancholy like sleep
Roam from your cheekbones, what then?
Should you disown melancholy
What then would become of fidelity?

There might not be -

If you were to glance up now
- You will not glance up now -
You would see me as I am:
A tiger on the wall;
Black hat, hornrims;
Flesh, bone, fur, lip;
A brace of eyes;
Brandy glaring out through every pore.

My sweetest wife,
How you must hate me.

You and I in our green world
Of green pain;
Potted plants among the potted plants;
You in your brown haute couture frock,
I in my brown shop coat;
Knees of clay.

The rooftops - not the bridges -
Of Paris far below.

A SELF-PORTRAIT
William Leech

Draughts

Solids and liquids;
Bodies and souls;
Thread.

Grand Canal Basin:
Belly of water
By a buckle
All held in.

I have got a pain
In my gut:
Your move.

It is all a blue bag - as the Tailor used say.
We have seen Eternity and it is mortal.

DRAUGHTS
Jack B. Yeats

IN THE TRAM

Jack B. Yeats

In The Tram

No one wanted him; he was outcast from life's feast.
- *A Painful Case*

I am afraid - I confide in my doctor -
After the operation for my duodenal ulcer
That when I am discharged from hospital
I will not be able to cope with the isolation;
That my wife having left me for her brother-in-law
And being myself a middle aged country man
With a clerical position in the city waterworks
With no close friends or relations or acquaintances
I will have no choice but to prostrate myself
Under a train at Sydney Parade
Or in my overcoat with the velour collar
Go for a late night swim in the River Dodder
With stones in my pockets.

The doctor - a burly blustering Kerryman -
Plunges his thumbs into his pinstripe waistcoat:
'Self-pity's slurry, I will not allow it, wallower you.
What you must do when you leave hospital
Is learn to ride the trams.
I appreciate that you are an outcast in Dublin
But once you have learned how to ride the trams
You will have penetrated the secret code of city life.
You have no idea the numbers of unattached women
Who use the trams but I have the statistics.
At least 72% of the women riding the trams
Are in want of a man, especially the married women.
But obviously also the unmarried women.
All you have to do is ride lots of trams, lots of them,
And Bob's your uncle, Nan's your aunt,
You will have a woman in no time.

'Personally I recommend the Lucan Route
Under the Phoenix Park Walls, the Knockmaroon Gate,

But what route you choose is a matter for yourself.
For all I know your needs might be best catered for
On the Dun Laoghaire Route.
The South Side is *terra incognita* to me
But that it is *terra firma* my registrars do assure me.
Your difficulty will be in selecting the right woman.
The crux will be cranking up
A *sacra conversazione*, so to speak, with the appropriate lady:
It is likely, I must warn you, that she will be living alone
With her only child - her grown-up daughter.'

As I sit bolt upright alone on the tram, a solitary epitome,
I endeavour to imagine what it must be like to be the tram driver
Glancing back over his shoulder into the laughing faces of three women
Under tinted ventilators
All handbags and conspiracy,
How as a trio they remind him of high tide at Bulloch Harbour:
Beyond them, across an empty expanse of ocean
- An empty seat can be an eternity -
The single sail of a solitary gent,
His hat featherless.

Glancing back over his shoulder, the tram driver
Glances a dray,
Brakes, and I am tipped up, over and out of my seat.
The three women slide back down along the rexine,
Collapse on top of me in a cafuffle and for seconds
I am smothered in petticoats - a swansong come true.
I have always had a yen for petticoats.
Their female voices. I could listen to it all day.
Heat and light. I dare not look around.
I feel so cold myself although it is the month of April
And thirty years past puberty.
I would not recognise my own voice if I heard it,
I do not think. It is 1923. I would say
I have about another seventeen years to live
Or seventeen minutes. I am going crazy -
Crazy without women.

Flower Girl, Dublin

Afternoons in winter
I sit in Robert Roberts Café
Watching men and women,
Especially women.
I am crazy about women.

Just because I am a man without a woman
Does not mean that I have no interest in women.
In fact I am preoccupied with fundamentally nothing else.
I read all of Nietzsche when I was seventeen.
Then it was time to grow up.

Would you please hose some of your hot liquid into me?
Mother of five to boy at coffee dispenser.
She must be forty at least but as she sips her grounds
- Her Costa Rican grounds -
As she slowly smacks her lips
Trickling her tonguetip along her liprim
She is a girl not yet nineteen
Haughty as an Englishwoman in Shanghai.
She is wearing a red cloche hat, grey wool overcoat,
Black low high-heel shoes.

I see in today's newspaper a black-and-white photograph
Of a woman in a black mini-skirt at the opening
Of the Séan McSweeney Retrospective last night
(There is a man who can paint - not many can
Since the Great Yeat died in 1957).

But much as that photo causes a stir in me
- An abstract stir in me -
It is as nothing compared to that glimpse of ankle
- Sheer ankle -
Of the mother of five in the red cloche hat
- Would you please hose some of your hot liquid into me?

FLOWER GIRL, DUBLIN
Jack B. Yeats

Time to go - home. I dally to loiter
In the doorway of the café semaphoring to myself
In the shopwindow opposite, my bowler hat,
My frock coat, my gleaming galoshes.
A flower girl with a single red rose in her hands
Is passing the time of day with the mother of five
Not making any particular pitch to sell.

Timorousness entices me to my right
But I know, Jack, I know
I should step briskly to my left,
Proffer the single red rose to the mother of five,
Nail my colours to the mast.
Will I or won't I?
And give all my loose change to the flower girl -
All my loose change?

NO FLOWERS
Jack B. Yeats

No Flowers

I

The day of my wife's funeral
I cycled behind the hearse
On my Hercules with dropped handlebars
All the way up to Mount Jerome
And back again.

I had a drink on my own
In The Waterloo House
In Baggot Street.
I was elated.
But after three glasses of claret
I was composed,
Ready for the improvisation.

I walked out into the night
Up to Baggot Street Bridge
Ready for the improvisation.
I walked straight through the locked
Glass door of Bord Fáilte.
When I got to my feet
I was a glass man.

I crept off in a stoop,
A stoop with the cream
Skimmed off its milk,
A bird cut out of glass,
Up along the canal,
No flowers in my claws.

II

Singing the praises
Of water, of catwalks, of locks,
Of artisans,
Of the total absence
Of dogs at this time of night,
Of towpaths, of canal bank seats,
Of lanes, of bookshops, of women -
Of women at pianos alone in flats
Playing Field Nocturnes,
Of Mary Lavin's daughters in Lad Lane,
Of the Misses King and O'Flaherty in Parsons Bookshop,
Of Michael Kane at his window in Waterloo Road.

My trousers are cut.
My jacket is cut.
I am walking up the middle of the canal
Up to my shinbones in water.
I am walking on my knees
Acquiring humility.
I like walking on my knees
Acquiring humility.
Humility is not endless.

No flowers on my knees
But the body of a bicycle
Which I hold up aloft:
Her darling head.
Are you ready for your new life, my love?
Your old frame back?

The Cavalier's Farewell To His Steed

Farewell to Poetry!

Striding out!
Striding out of the picture!

Poetry split open my skull:
All saddlebags and rattlesnakes.

Blinkers, sensitive
Egos, reams.

Buskins, stock,
Similes, themes.

Parasites, bits
And pieces, tippex.

Farewell to morality.
Farewell to identity.

What's left of me striding out:
Having been eaten alive.

Horseflesh. Veins.
Bladder. Brains.

Striding out not with my belovèd wife
As all my life I pined,

Not with my compatible woman
But alone.

Striding out!
Striding out the tightrope of a suburban street.

Snowdrops!
Daffodils!

THE CAVALIER'S FAREWELL TO HIS STEED
Jack B. Yeats

Farewell to my donkey.
Farewell to my song.

Above the pines the moon was slowly drifting.
The river sang below;
The dim Sierras, far beyond, uplifting
Their minarets of snow.

To be free!
Such grief in my stride.

To have shed my last poem.
Never again to be beholden.

Blood transfusion;
Watching somebody else's blood drip into me.

After Poetry, what?
A job, maybe, in transport.

The Bay of Fundy;
Last Train to Tokyo.

Japan, Maine;
Yourcenar, Mishima.

Sheep's legs awaiting me
Across the sea.

Farewell to Poetry!

GRIEF

Jack B. Yeats

Grief

I

I am a man;
All that is human is alien to me.

I insert my penis gun into your mouth and
- As the quaint old mantra has it -
'Blow your brains out'.

How I delight to behold
At evening by the campfire on the seashore
After our games of softball
The wild, wild hedgerows
Lambent with your dripping brains:

Oilily -
When I drop my Judaeo-Christian trousers,
Spread out my legs across the Islamic sky,
Drop my droppings on you.

What I admire most about myself,
What I most cherish
In my children's bedrooms
As I lull their cradles,
Is my own ordure.

A man's own ordure
Is the basis of culture;
In the hi-tech of my ordure
Ticks the future of my futurelessness.

My golden locks
Are things of the past.

I am a man;
All that is human is alien to me.

II

I was on the Dublin-Cork train minding my own business
When a not-so-young man opposite me - about the same age as myself -
Put down his paper and asked me without a by-your-leave
'What class of occupation are you in yourself?'
To my surprise I answered him:
'I am an art gallery attendant.'

I can still hear myself saying it:
'I am an art gallery attendant' -
Has a ring to it.
The beautiful thing was that it shut him up.
We were only pulling out of Kildare
But he did not open his mouth again
The whole way down to Cork.

I am an art gallery attendant
In the National Gallery of Ireland.
I am the man
Who sits under 'Grief'
At the head of the Gallery
Watching fleets of feet paddling towards me.
If anyone asks me what 'Grief' means
I say I do not know what 'Grief' means.
That is the truth. I do not know what 'Grief' means.
I do not think anyone knows what 'Grief' means.
It is a pretty picture - that is all I know about 'Grief'
After having sat under it for twenty-five years
And I think that is all anybody knows about 'Grief'.

Another thing that I do not understand
Is people who make a racket with their footwear on the parquet.
It never fails to grate on my nerves.
What's in it for a body to wantonly introduce
Noise into a place of worship?

It's like people who say you can support wars
When obviously there is no way you can support wars
Or people who see fit to bite hardboiled sweets in cinemas.
I suppose it's something inherent in society and the individual,
Crowds and power.
That is what I often think
Sitting here under 'Grief'.

People often ask me also the way to the Restaurant.
By the time they have finished asking me
They have spotted it and they apologise
For having asked me in the first place.
By this time they have caught a glimpse of 'Grief'.
They stop in their tracks. They stare up at it
Like as if they have seen a horse come through the wall.
All of us hanging about in the parade ring at a race meeting.
Nervously they approach it and at the last moment they make
A dive into the corner to sniff the label.
They canter up and down the length of the picture
Before standing back out again in the middle
Like connections in the middle of the parade ring
Pleased with themselves to be at the centre of the picture,
Yet anxious to get back outside again and to watch
- Or not to watch, as the case may be - from a safe distance.
'Grief'. I scratch my chin. They scamper off for their coleslaw.
Punters scoff a lot of coleslaw in the National Gallery of Ireland.

Index

26

Man With Two Daughters, c.1565
Giambattista Moroni (c.1520/25-1578)
oil on canvas
126 x 98 cms.
N.G.I. 105

28

Cain And Abel, c.1620
Circle of Riminaldi, (1586-1630/31)
oil on canvas
200 x 147.5 cms.
N.G.I. 1667

31

Interior With Figures
Nicolaes de Gyselaer (1583-before 1659)
oil on panel
36 x 56 cms.
N.G.I. 327

32

Acis And Galatea, c.1629/31
Nicolas Poussin (1594-1665)
oil on canvas
98 x 137 cms.
N.G.I. 814

34

The Veneration Of The Eucharist, c.1630
Jacob Jordaens (1593-1678)
oil on canvas
285 x 235.1 cms.
N.G.I. 46

37

Kitchen Maid With The Supper At Emmaus, c.1618
Diego Velázquez de Silva (1599-1660)
oil on canvas
55 x 118 cms.
N.G.I. 4538

40

Saint Cecilia
Iacopo Vignali (1592-1664)
oil on canvas
140 x 145 cms.
N.G.I. 183

44

The Levite And His Concubine At Gibeah, c.1650
Jan Victors (c.1619-1676)
oil on canvas
103.6 x 136.5 cms.
N.G.I. 879

48

The Sleeping Shepherdess, c.1658
Jan Baptist Weenix (1621-c.1660-61)
oil on canvas
72.5 x 61.1 cms.
N.G.I. 511

50

The Riding School, 1678
Karel Dujardin (c.1622-1678)
oil on canvas
60.2 x 73.5 cms.
N.G.I. 544

54

Lady Mary Wortley Montagu, 1720s
Charles Jervas (c.1675-1739)
oil on canvas
214.5 x 126 cms.
N.G.I. 4342

56

The Dilettanti, 1736
Cornelis Troost (1696-1750)
oil on panel
68 x 58 cms.
N.G.I. 497

60

Bishop Robert Clayton And His Wife Katherine, 1730s
James Latham (1696-1747)
oil on canvas
128 x 175 cms.
N.G.I. 4370

62

Joseph Leeson, 1744
Pompeo Girolamo Batoni (1708-1787)
oil on canvas
137 x 102 cms.
N.G.I. 701

64

An Interior With Members Of A Family, 1750s
Philip Hussey (1713-1783)
oil on canvas
62 x 76 cms.
N.G.I. 4304

68

The Earl Of Bellamont, c.1774
Joshua Reynolds (1723-1792)
oil on canvas
245 x 162 cms.
N.G.I. 216

70

Mrs Congreve With Her Children, 1782
Philip Reinagle (1749-1833)
oil on canvas
80.5 x 106 cms.
N.G.I. 676

72

Bishop Of Derry With His Granddaughter, c.1788
Hugh Douglas Hamilton (c.1739-1808)
oil on canvas
230 x 199 cms.
N.G.I. 4350

76

Sir John And Lady Clerk Of Penicuik, c.1791
Henry Raeburn (1756-1823)
oil on canvas
145 x 206 cms.
N.G.I. 4530

80

Fish, 1944
Albert Power (c.1883-1945)
marble
48 cms. ht.
N.G.I. 8090

85

Thomas Moore In His Study At Sloperton Cottage
English School (19th century)
oil on panel
30 x 36 cms.
N.G.I. 4312

86

Bathers Surprised, 1852-53
William Mulready (1786-1863)
oil on panel
59 x 44 cms.
N.G.I. 611

88

Demosthenes On The Seashore, 1859
Eugène Delacroix (1798-1863)
oil on paper laid on panel
47.5 x 58 cms.
N.G.I. 964

90

Marguerite In Church, c.1861
James Tissot (1836-1902)
oil on canvas
50.2 x 75.5 cms.
N.G.I. 4280

94

The Meeting On The Turret Stairs, 1864
Frederic William Burton (1816-1900)
watercolour on paper
95.5 x 60.8 cms.
N.G.I. 2358

96

A Group Of Cavalry In The Snow, 1876
Ernest Meissonier (1815-1891)
oil on panel
37.5 x 47 cms.
N.G.I. 4263

98

Boy Eating Cherries, 1895
Pierre Bonnard (1867-1947)
oil on board
52 x 41 cms.
N.G.I. 4356

100

A Man Seated On A Sofa
Edouard Vuillard (1868-1940)
gouache on card
41 x 53.9 cms.
N.G.I. 3017

104

The Knucklebone Player
Gustav Natorp (1836-after 1898)
bronze
54 cms. ht.
N.G.I. 8084

106

Dawn, Connemara, 1920s
Paul Henry (1876-1958)
oil on canvas
47 x 62 cms.
N.G.I. 1234

110

Supper Time, 1912
Patrick Tuohy (1894-1930)
pencil and watercolour with white highlights on paper
50 x 70 cms.
N.G.I. 3306

112

Self-Portrait In The Artist's Studio, 1920
Moyra Barry (1886-1960)
oil on canvas
30.4 x 25.5 cms.
N.G.I. 4366

114
Man Walking The Stairs, 1922-23
Chaim Soutine (1893-1943)
oil on canvas
81.5 x 65 cms.
N.G.I. 4485

120
A Portrait Of The Artist's Wife, c.1920
William Leech (1881-1968)
oil on canvas
75 x 60 cms.
N.G.I. 1915

122
A Self-Portrait, 1966
William Leech (1881-1968)
oil on canvas
64 x 56 cms.
N.G.I. 1914

123
Draughts, 1922
Jack B. Yeats (1871-1957)
oil on panel
23 x 36 cms.
N.G.I. 1407

124
In The Tram, 1923
Jack B. Yeats (1871-1957)
oil on panel
23 x 36 cms.
N.G.I. 1408

128
Flower Girl, Dublin, 1926
Jack B. Yeats (1871-1957)
oil on canvas
46 x 61 cms.
N.G.I. 1905

130
No Flowers, 1945
Jack B. Yeats (1871-1957)
oil on canvas
61 x 92 cms.
N.G.I. 4031

134
The Cavalier's Farewell To His Steed, 1949
Jack B. Yeats (1871-1957)
oil on board
36 x 46 cms.
N.G.I. 1374

136
Grief, 1951
Jack B. Yeats (1871-1957)
oil on canvas
102 x 153 cms.
N.G.I. 1769

Among Paul Durcan's published works are:

The Selected Paul Durcan, Blackstaff Press, Belfast, 1982
The Berlin Wall Café, Blackstaff Press, Belfast, 1985
Going Home To Russia, Blackstaff Press, Belfast, 1987
Jesus and Angela, Blackstaff Press, Belfast, 1988
Daddy, Daddy, Blackstaff Press, Belfast, 1990